Forever Remembered ™

Compiled by
Dan Zadra with Marcia Woodard

Designed by
Kobi Yamada and Steve Potter

COM·PEN´·DI·UM ™
Incorporated

Acknowledgements

These quotations, verses, and reflections were gathered lovingly but unscientifically over several years and/or were contributed by many friends or bereavement organizations. Some arrived—and survived in our files—on scraps of paper and may therefore be imperfectly worded or attributed. To the authors, contributors, and original sources, our thanks, and where appropriate, our apologies.
—The Editors.

With Special Thanks To

Jason Aldrich, Gerry Baird, Jay Baird, Bill Barrett, Justi Baumgardt, Neil Beaton, Rob & Beth Bingham, Cindy Cothern, Doug Cruickshank, Jim Darragh, Josie & Rob Estes, Jack Gordon, Holly Hughes, Jennifer Hurwitz, Dick Kamm, Beth Keane, Liam Lavery, Jim Letson, Connie McMartin, Jay Musselman, Jim & Teri O'Brien, Janet Potter & Family, Diane Roger, Cristal Spurr, Floyd Scott, Rich Sells, Sam Sundquist, Pat Wicks, Jenica Wilkie, Heidi Wills, George Woodard, Robert & Val Yamada, Tote Yamada, Anne Zadra, Augie & Rosie Zadra, August & Arline Zadra and the entire staff of Service Corporation International (SCI).

Credits

Compiled by Dan Zadra with Marcia Woodard

Designed by Kobi Yamada and Steve Potter

Dedicated to Jeffrey Hurwitz

A Gift for the Grieving Heart

OUR GRIEF ALWAYS BRINGS A GIFT...

When one of his classmates died, an eight-year-old friend visited the boy's home one day after school. "What did you say?" asked his mother gently when the child returned? "Nothing," he replied. "I just sat on his mom's lap and helped her cry."

🍃

When someone we care about loses a loved one, we too want to help—but how? Some things we just can't do for each other. We can't believe for each other; faith is so sacred and so personal. We can't restore the loved one to life, or turn back the clock, or eliminate the pain. Usually, we can't even find the right words to express the feelings overflowing in our hearts.

*B*ut we can do what the children do. We can bring the one gift that requires no words, and which always, always triumphs over death. Quietly, fervently, faithfully, we can bring our love.

*T*his, then, is our gift to the grieving heart. Let the messages in this little book remind you that death can never extinguish our love. It cannot suppress our faith. It cannot restrain our hopes. It cannot destroy our compassion. It cannot end our friendship. It cannot tarnish our memories. It cannot silence our courage. It cannot conquer our soul. It cannot vanquish our spirit. And it cannot steal eternal life.

Dan Zadra

$\mathcal{I}$ am here.
Let's heal together.

—$\mathcal{A}$ friend

$\mathcal{I}$ did not come to comfort you;
only God and time can do that; but
I did come to say how deeply and tenderly
I feel for you in your sorrow.

—$\mathcal{B}y$ $\mathcal{Y}our$ $\mathcal{S}ide$

"I'll cry with you,"

she whispered,

until we run out of tears.

Even if it's forever.

We'll do it together."

There it was...a simple

promise of connection.

The loving alliance of

grief and hope that

blesses both our breaking

apart and our coming

together again.

— Molly Fumia, Safe Passage

$\mathcal{E}$ mpathy is your pain
I feel in my heart.

—Hospice Volunteer

$\mathcal{T}$ hank you for letting me talk
and letting me cry.
Thank you for cheerful hello's
and tearful goodbye's.
Thank you for asking questions
and saying her name.
Thank you for not understanding
but sharing my pain.

—Jacqueline M. Savageau, Unite Notes Newsletter

Forever
Remembered

8

I was sitting, torn by grief. Someone came
and talked to me of God's dealings, of
why it happened, of why my loved one had
died, of hope beyond the grave. He talked
constantly. He said things I knew were true.
I was unmoved, except to wish he'd go away.
He finally did.
Another came and sat beside me.
He didn't talk. He didn't ask me leading
questions. He just sat beside me for an hour
and more, listening when I said something,
answered briefly, prayed simply, left.
I was moved. I was comforted. I hated
to see him go.

—Joe Bayly

The healing began
when a friend embraced me,
leaving some of his tears on my cheek.

—*Time Remembered*

In Asian countries,
one can still find delicate tear vases
used by mourners. The tears shed into the
little vases are considered sacred.
The tear bottles are kept and often buried
with the person mourned. Even if our
tears are for ourselves, for *our* ache of
loneliness, for *our* pain of loss, they are still
sacred, for they are tears of our love.

—*Rabbi Jack Stern, Jr.*

*N*eeded: A strong, deep person wise enough
to allow me to grieve in the depth of who I am,
and strong enough to hear my pain without
turning away.

I need someone who believes that the sun will
rise again, but who does not fear my darkness.
Someone who can point out the rocks in my way
without making me a child by carrying me.
Someone who can stand in thunder and watch
the lightning, and believe in a rainbow.

Fr. Joe Mahoney,
Concerns of Police Survivors Newsletter

It's okay to scream
at God. He can take it.
—Earl Grollman

Cancer is not God's will. The death
of a child is not God's will. Deaths from
automobile accidents are not God's will.
The only God worth believing in does not
cause the tragedies but lovingly comes
into the anguish with us.
— Madeline L'Engle

For I know the plans I have for you;
plans to comfort you and not to harm you,
plans to give you hope and a future.
—Jeremiah 29:11

The conventional explanation, that God sends us the burden because He knows that we are strong enough to handle it, has it all wrong. Fate, not God, sends us the anguish. When we try to deal with it, we find out that we are not strong. We are weak; we get tired, we get angry, overwhelmed. We begin to wonder how we will ever make it through all the years. But when we reach the limits of our own strength and courage, something unexpected happens. We find reinforcement coming from a source outside of ourselves. And in the knowledge that we are not alone, that God is on our side, we manage to go on.

—Harold S. Kushner,
   When Bad Things Happen to Good People

$\mathcal{T}$o everything
there is a season, and a time
to every purpose under heaven.

—*Ecclesiastes 3:1*

$\mathcal{N}$othing is terminal,
just transitional.

—*Dr. Robert Schuller*

$\mathcal{G}$od has written
the promise of resurrection, not
in books alone, but in every
leaf in springtime.

—*Martin Luther*

"Then what has been the reason for all of this?"
Freddie continued to question. "Why were
we here at all if we only have to fall and die?"

Daniel answered in his matter-of-fact way,
"It's been about the sun and the moon.
It's been about happy times together.
It's been about the shade and the old people
and the children. It's been about colors in Fall.
It's been about seasons. Isn't that enough?"

That afternoon, in the golden light of
dusk, Daniel let go. He fell effortlessly.
He seemed to smile peacefully as he fell.
"Good-bye for now Freddie," he said.

— Leo Buscaglia, Ph.D.,
    The Fall of Freddie the Leaf

The aim, if reached or not,
makes great the life.

—Robert Browning

❧

Tell me not in mournful numbers
Life is but an empty dream!
Lives of great men all remind us
We can make our lives sublime,
And, departing, leave behind us
Footprints in the sands of time.

—Henry Wadsworth Longfellow

❧

Every action of our lives
touches a chord that vibrates in Eternity.

—Edwin Hubbel Chapin

"Human beings do not live forever. We live less than the time it takes to blink an eye, if we measure our lives against eternity. So it may be asked what value is there to a human life. There is so much pain in the world. What does it mean to have to suffer so much if our lives are nothing more than the blink of an eye?" He paused again, his eyes misty now, then went on. "I learned a long time ago, that a blink of an eye in itself is nothing. But the eye that blinks, that is something. A span of life is nothing. But the man who lives that span, he is something. He can fill that tiny span with meaning, so its quality is immeasurable though its quantity may be insignificant."

—Chaim Potok

Is this the end? I know it cannot be,
Our ships shall sail upon another sea;
New islands yet shall break upon our sight,
New continents of love and truth and might.
—John White Chadwick

I am looking with an eager interest into
the "undiscovered country" and leaving this
earth with no regret, except that I have not
accomplished more work. But I don't doubt
we shall keep on working.
—Helen Hunt

In a harbor, two ships sailed—one setting forth on a voyage, the other coming home to port. Everyone cheered the ship going out, but the ship sailing in was scarcely noticed. To this, a wise man said, "Do not rejoice over a ship setting out to sea, for you cannot know what terrible storms it may encounter. Rejoice rather over the ship that has safely reached port and brings its passengers home in peace." And this is the way of the world: When a child is born, all rejoice; when someone dies, all weep. We should do the opposite. For no one can tell what trials await a newborn child; but when a mortal dies in peace, we should rejoice, for he has completed a long journey, and there is no greater boon than to leave this world with the imperishable crown of a good name.

—The Talmud

Believing where we cannot prove.

—Alfred Lord Tennyson

I never spoke to God
Nor visited in heaven;
Yet certain am I of the spot
As if the chart were given.

—Emily Dickinson

Seems it strange that thou shouldst live forever?
Is it less strange that thou shouldst live at all?
This is a miracle; and that no more.

—Edward Young

I don't care what they say with their mouths—everybody knows that something is eternal. And it ain't houses, and it ain't names, and it ain't earth, and it ain't even stars—everybody knows in their bones that something is eternal, and that something has to do with human beings. All the greatest people ever lived have been telling us that for five thousand years and yet you'd be surprised how people are always losing hold of it. There's something way down deep that's eternal about every human being.

Thornton Wilder,
Our Town

The day I die I can say I have finished my day's work. But I cannot say I have finished my life. My day's work will begin again the next morning.

—*Victor Hugo*

I have seen death too often to believe in death. It is not an ending—but a withdrawal as one who finishes a long journey, stills the motor, turns off the light, steps from his car and walks up the path to the home that awaits him.

—*Don Blanding*

Death is nothing at all—I have only slipped away into the next room. I am I, and you are you. Whatever we were to each other, that we still are. Call me by my old familiar name, speak to me in the easy way you always used. Wear no forced air of solemnity or sorrow. Laugh as we always laughed at the little jokes we enjoyed together. Play, smile, think of me, pray for me. Let my name be ever the household word that it always was. Life means all that it ever meant. There is absolutely unbroken continuity....Why should I be out of mind because I am out of sight? I am waiting for you—for an interval—somewhere near, just around the corner. All is well.

—Henry Scott Holland

Out of love comes suffering;
out of suffering comes love.
That is the mystery.

—*Louise Cordana*

🍂

When you are sorrowful,
look again in your heart and you shall see
in truth you are weeping for that which
has been your delight.

—*Kahil Gibran,*
The Prophet

🍂

All who have been touched by beauty are
touched by sorrow at its passing.

—*Louise Cordana*

Forever
Remembered

Only the person who is incapable of love is
entirely free of the possibility of grief.
In the words of a dying man:

"The agony is great
and yet I will stand it.
Had I not loved so very much,
I would not hurt so much.
But goodness knows I would not want
to diminish that precious love by one fraction.
I will hurt and I will be grateful for it.
For it bears witness to
the depth of our meanings
and for that I will be eternally grateful."

—From Scotty, Hospice Chaplain

We have loved the stars too fondly
to be fearful of the night.

—Epitaph for John and Phoebe Brashear

No light that was born in love
can ever be extinguished.

—Darcie D. Sims, Ph.D.,
Bereavement Magazine

There is only one way for you
to live without grief in your lifetime; that is
to exist without love. Your grief represents
your humanness, just as your love does.

—Carol Staudacher

I remember the first minute that Carl (Sagan) and I fell in love. The gates of the world opened up, but at the same moment I had a sense of awesome liabilities. When you love someone that much and you are that happy, you know that if something happens to the other person you will be smashed. Still, I have learned in the last six months that when you love someone with your heart and soul, you are left with something that is enough to sustain you. Loving on what is essentially a tiny pale blue dot, as Carl called the Earth, and having that soaring experience is what makes the vastness bearable.

—Annie Druyan, remembering her husband

$\mathcal{Y}$our heart has brought
great joy to many. Those hearts
can never forget you.
—*Flavia Weeden*

$\mathcal{B}$ut when God sent you to me
He never said that you were mine,
That I could keep you always—
Only borrowed for a time.

Now, He's called you home,
I'm sad and I shed tears.
Yet I'm glad He loaned you to me
And we had these many years.
—*Edna T. Burch,*
"Missing You"

We are gathered together in her memory.

If you seek her memorial, look about you: it's in the hearts of her family, in the faces of her children, in her writings and in her home. Life has been given and life has been taken away. Life and death are one, even as the river and the sea are one. Death is only a horizon, and a horizon is but the limit of our sight. Since we know nothing of death except that it comes to all, it is not reasonable to be sad for the person who has died The sorrow that once I felt for myself, in my loss, now has been transformed to a rich memory of a woman I loved and the ways we traveled through the world together.

— George A. Crile, Jr., in memory of his wife, Jane

There are some people who, when they die,
the whole world seems depopulated.
—Alphonse de Lamartine

Some die without having really lived,
while others continue to live,
in spite of the fact that they have died.
— Unknown

It's such an act of
optimism to get through a day and
enjoy it and laugh and do all that
without thinking about dying.
What spirit human beings have!

—Gilda Radner
(From San Diego Hospice)

Forever
Remembered

30

I don't know why God makes people and then takes them back while they're still having fun with the life He gave them in the first place. Just like I don't know if I'm supposed to celebrate the fact that Gilda [Radner] was in my life, or feel cheated that she's not here anymore. But even though her body grew to betray her, spirits just don't die. And that's what Gilda was.

—Alan Zweibel,
*Bunny Bunny: Gilda Radner:
A Sort of Love Story*

You may forget
with whom you laughed,
but you will never forget
with whom you wept.

—Carie O'Leary

There is joy in heaven
when a tear of sorrow is shed in the
presence of a truly understanding heart.
And heaven will never forget that joy.

—Charles Malik

In time we can accept a great loss if we have
somebody loving us through it. God sends friends
and companions to love and support us.

—Dr. Robert Schuller

In the beginning, there is a whole year of those terrible "firsts"—his birthday, your birthday, your anniversary, all the holidays. Each time one came and went, however, it was a small victory, achieved with the help of those around me. My mother and my dogs formed the inner circle. Then there were the friends who set about putting pieces back together, each in his or her own way. They know who they are, and I'm deeply grateful.

—Betty White, actress, recalling her husband,
Allen Ludden
Here We Go Again

Our grief always brings a gift.
It's the gift of greater sensitivity and
compassion for others. We learn to rise above
our own grief by reaching out and
lessening the grief of others.

—Dr. Robert Schuller

If I can stop one Heart from breaking,
I shall not live in vain.
If I can ease one Life the Aching
Or cool one Pain
Or help one fainting Robin
Unto his Nest again,
I shall not live in Vain.

—Emily Dickinson

Tom pledged his love to me and I gave my love to him; I was a bride and I thought I knew what love was. Our infant son smiled at me when I sang to him; I was a young mother and I thought I knew what love was. Our adopted baby girl was placed in our arms; I was older and I thought I knew what love was. For seven years our children's laughter rang through our home; I was middle-aged and I thought I knew what love was. I looked into her face when God called her back home and I held her hand to say good-bye; I lost my little girl and I thought I forgot what love was. But eight lives were changed, eight people were given a second chance to live because we donated our daughter's organs. Now I know what love is.

—Rae Ann Reichert, "What Love Is"

God is closest
to those with broken hearts.

—Jewish Saying

A wife who loses a husband is called a widow.
A husband who loses a wife is called a widower.
A child who loses his parents is called an orphan.
But in Yiddish they say there is no word for a parent
who loses a child. That's how awful the loss is.

—Jay Neugeboren,
"An Orphan's Tale," Loving Arms Newsletter

Most people don't know how
brave they really are.

—R.E. Chambers

A message to my wife:

The years of our marriage are few when measured
against a lifetime. We have encountered joy and
shared confidence in our future. We have known
hope's ending and have borne the death of dreams.
We have together been diminished. Even minor
aspirations have eluded our grasp in the cruel
shadow of the loss of our child. Yet we still share
our lives. And though the brightness we once knew
has fled, we have grown enough to sense a return
of laughter—an uplifting to shatter the dimness,
to remind us that tomorrow will come and dreams
may again be born.

—Don Hackett, Friends for Survival, Inc.

All the darkness in the world
cannot extinguish the light
of a single candle.

— *Maria Gautier*

Time has healed me,
but time has not made me forget.

— *Janis Heil*

Glow brightly, little light,
and send my message:
"I will love you, never forget you,
always be with you."

— *Jeri Gingham*

I have grown to believe that even as these losses
have broken me, so can they heal me....
When someone I love dies, I buy a candle.
There are twelve across my mantle now:
one for my father, one for my mother, one
for my daughter, two for my grandfathers,
and seven for my babies who were born too
soon. It is a simple, comforting act to light
them in reverent remembrance of each life.
Whenever anyone stops to count these candles,
the question I am most frequently asked is,
"How did you do it? How did you survive?"
My usual answer: "I don't know."

—Dana Gensler, "Twelve Candles,"
LARGO Newsletter

Faith is the bird that feels the light
when the dawn is still dark.

—Rabindranath Tagore

Sad soul,
take comfort nor forget,
The sunrise never failed us yet.

—Celia Laighton Thaxter

In the depth of winter,
I finally learned that within me
lies an invincible summer.

—Albert Camus

Forever
Remember

40

"You will not always hurt like this."
These words are true.
If they do not reach your heart today,
do not reject them:
keep them in your mind.

One morning, not tomorrow perhaps,
but the day after tomorrow,
or the month after next month...
One morning the dawn will wake you
with the inconceivable surprise:
Your grief will have lost
one small moment of its force.

Be ready for the time
when you can feel for yourself
that these words are true:
"You will not always hurt like this."

—Sascha,
"True Words," Wintersun

Absent in body, but present in spirit.

—Corinthians 1:3

The heart hath its own memory,
like the mind.
And in it are enshrined the precious keepsakes,
into which is wrought the giver's loving thought.

—H. W. Longfellow

Death ends a life, but death does not end a
relationship. If we allow ourselves to be still,
and if we take responsibility for our grief,
the grief becomes as polished and luminous and
mysterious as death itself. When it does, we learn
to love anew, not only the one who has died.
We learn to love anew those who yet live.

—Julius Lester

Dealing with the grief of the sudden and unexpected death of my husband, and the sadness of being unable to touch him, became overwhelming until I realized that his essence—his kindness, love, strength, sensitivity, and goodness remained. I realized that, although the physical person was sought, it was not the physical persona who had captured my heart. It was his essence which had united with me. Those intangible characteristics endure. From this knowledge came the ability to reopen the closed door to my heart, which then became the container wherein is stored his non-physical being. He dwells there in my heart, and his generosity continues as he prods me to make room for others.

—Patricia S. Saloga, "Container for Love"

$\mathcal{L}$ove like ours can never die!

—*Rudyard Kipling*

This is not the end, we'll meet again
God's promise will be kept,
But all the same, I feel no shame
in all the tears I've wept.

With God's own grace, I'll see your face
when it is my turn to die.
I loved you so, just that, no more;
for now, I'll say goodbye.

—*Forest R. Whatley*

Forever Remember

44

How do I love thee?

Let me count the ways.

I love thee to the depth and breadth

and height

My soul can reach, when feeling out

of sight

for the ends of Being and ideal

Grace...

I love thee with the breath,

Smiles, tears, of all my life!—and, if

God choose,

I shall but love thee better after

death.

—Elizabeth Barrett Browning,
Sonnets from the Portuguese

If you should hear a song,
out in the meadow loud and clear,
have no fear—he is there.
The melody heard is that of love,
and those who listen hear it true.

— Unknown

There's not an hour
Of day or dreaming night but I am with thee;
There's not a breeze but whispers of thy name,
And not a flower that sleeps beneath the moon
But in its fragrance tells a
tale of thee.

—Barry Cornwall

My very dear Sarah,   July 14, 1861

My love for you is deathless...but if I do not return, never forget how much I love you. And when my last breath escapes me on the battle field, it will whisper your name. But, Oh Sarah! If the dead can come back to this earth and flit unseen around those they have loved, I shall always be near you; in the gladdest days and the darkest nights, always, always. And if there be a soft breeze upon your cheek, it shall be my breath, as the cool air fans your throbbing temple, it shall be my spirit passing by. Sarah do not mourn me dead; think I am gone and wait for thee, for we shall meet again.

—A letter from Major Sullivan Ballou, who died at the first Battle of Bull Run

$\mathcal{W}$e are told they will be replaced.
This only means that other such men will take
their places. The three cannot be replaced.
There never was a replaceable human being.

—Eric Sevareid,
for American astronauts Virgil Grissom,
Edward White and Roger Chaffee

$\mathcal{I}$ say good-bye to you, hero, and ask you
to rest in peace, and think about us, and miss
us, as down here we love you so very much.
I imagine angels are accompanying you now
and I ask them to take care of you,
because you deserve their protection.

—Noa Ben-Artzi Philosof,
eulogy for her grandfather Yitzhak Rabin

The world will little note, nor long remember, what we say here, but it can never forget what they did here. It is for us the living, rather, to be dedicated here to the unfinished work which they who fought here have thus far so nobly advanced. It is rather for us to be here dedicated to the great task remaining before us—that from these honored dead we take increased devotion to that cause for which they gave the last full measure of devotion— that we here highly resolve that these dead shall not have died in vain....

—Abraham Lincoln, The Gettysburg Address

$\mathcal{B}$ye and bye,
his Maker caught his eye.

—A waiter's epitaph in London

❧

$\mathcal{I}$ always remember an epitaph which
is in the cemetery at Tombstone, Arizona.
It says: "Here lies Jack Williams.
He done his damnedest." I think that is
the greatest epitaph a man can have.

—Harry S. Truman

❧

$\mathcal{G}$ravestone epitaph
requested by Erma Bombeck:
"Big deal! I'm used to dust."

—The Book of Life

The body of Benjamin Franklin,

Printer,

Like the Cover of an old Book,

Its Contents torn out,

And stript of its Lettering and Gilding

Lies here, Food for Worms

But the Work itself shall not be lost,

It will (as he believed) appear once more,

In a new and more beautiful Edition,

Corrected and amended

By the Author.

—*Epitaph on Benjamin Franklin's tombstone,*
written by himself

Do not neglect to honour his grave.

—Ecclesiastes 38:16

In love longing
I listen to the monk's bell.
I will never forget you
even for an interval
short as those between the bell notes.

—Izumi Shikibu

Visit often.
Light a candle in your soul, and place
a flower at the grave above her heart.

—Sasaki Yok

An old monk was once asked why he cared for ancient graves, and why he cleaned the stones to preserve the writings carved there. His reply was simple: "They still have their names. They will always have their names." A life infused with love has consequences that reach beyond time—ensuring that names, and places, and memories of what was still are, and always will be. They are not dead, can never die.

—Gregory and Suzanne Wolfe,
Climb High, Climb Far

G ive sorrow words.

— *William Shakespeare*

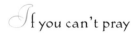

P rayer is not asking.
It is a longing of the soul.

— *Mahatma Gandhi*

I f you can't pray

as you want to,

pray as you can.

God knows what you mean.

— *Vance Havner*

Just one more Hi,
Just one more good-bye,
Just one more moment,
Just one more second.

Just one more hug,
Just one more tug,
Just one more kiss,
Just one more miss.

Just one more flower,
Just one more hour,
Just one more dance,
Just one more chance.

—Alise Ann Heimbecker, granddaughter of
Cpt. Phillip A. Heimbecker, Sr.,
killed in the line of duty June 11, 1993.
Concerns of Police Survivors Newsletter

Sweet miracle, to see how the largest burdens
are carried by the smallest children.

—Ardith James

Outside the church,
the adults huddled together
in the rain and cried.
Suddenly the children
spontaneously released
a big yellow balloon.
As it soared skyward,
the balloon somehow lifted
an immense weight
from the congregation.

—Thomas Baldwin, The Wisdom of Children

To the Brave Children:

It is easy to feel as though we, as children, are very small in this big world...but it is important to remember that we are not helpless or small. We have the power to talk to someone about how we feel.... Expressing yourself is very courageous, especially when the feelings you are expressing include sadness or confusion. All children who have experienced something tragically painful in our lives know what it's like to feel this way. Even by getting up every morning or coming to help support each other, we are showing ourselves that we are big.

—Caitlin Bernstein, Our House

$\mathcal{B}$lessed are they that mourn;
for they shall be comforted.

— *Matthew 5:4*

$\mathcal{G}$od comforts. He doesn't pity.
He picks us up, dries our tears, soothes our
fears, and lifts our thoughts beyond the hurt.

— *Dr. Robert Schuller*

$\mathcal{B}$e comforted.
You would not be seeking Him
if you had not found Him.

— *Pascal Pensees*

*Forever
Remember*

Lean on Me, child, and cry, I know your heart is broken. I called your loved one home today, he is with Me. Look to Me, child, and trust. I am acquainted with grief. Hold on to Me, child. I know the searing of your soul, and I will ease your pain. Keep your eyes on Me, child. I will not abandon you. Be comforted, My child. Your loved one is rejoicing in My presence. Someday, My child, you will be with Me, and see your loved one again, where you will know no tears, death or loneliness. I love you, dear child, and know your hurt... so lean on Me and cry.

— Donna Leonard, "Compassionate Christ,"
Twinless Twins Support Group Newsletter

When someone takes his own life,
we anguish that we should have known
enough to help. But only God knows
the weight of another's burden.

— *Mother Teresa of Calcutta*

A million times we've missed you,
A million times we've cried.
If love could have saved you,
You never would have died.

Things we feel most deeply,
Are the hardest things to say.
Our dearest one, we have loved you
In a very special way.

— *Unknown*

We all think of you so often, even when it hurts to remember. We are really lonely for your presence, and whenever we hear your songs, we still cry for you. We feel sad that you're not here to share so many events with us. That's when our mornings have no beginnings and our nights seem as long as winter. Yet we also know that, no matter what, we couldn't choose for you. We are learning to stop feeling responsible for your death. If we were responsible for you, you'd still be alive! We pray that you have peace. At the end of our days we look forward to being with you again.

—Fr. Arnaldo Pangrazzi, letter to a loved one who commits suicide, Friends for Survival, Inc.

There are many tears in the heart
that never reach the eyes.

— Unknown

But shall the angels call for him
much sooner than we've planned,
We'll brave the bitter grief that comes
and try to understand.

—Edgar Guest

Listen to a heart that is crying...
Because you can't see the tears.

— Mabelle Pittman

Forever
Remembe

62

I heard quite often "men don't cry"
Though no one ever told me why.
So when I fell and skinned a knee
No one came to comfort me.
And as I grew to reasoned years
I learned to stifle any tears.
No pain or setback could there be
Could wrest one single tear from me.
Then one long night I stood nearby
And helplessly watched my son die.
And quickly found to my surprise
That all that tearless talk was lies.
And still I cry and have no shame
I cannot play that "big boy" game,
And openly without remorse
I let my sorrow take its course.

—Ken Falk, Loving Arms Newsletter

God, give me guts.

—Eli Mygatt

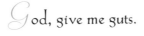

God has not promised skies always blue,
flower-strewn pathways all our lives through;
God has not promised sun without rain,
joy without sorrow, peace without pain.
But God has promised strength for the day,
rest for the labor, light for the way,
Grace for the trials, help from above,
unfailing sympathy, undying love.

—Kristone

I will take the leap of faith and peace;
I will let go and let God.

—Dana Fonseca

God grant me the serenity
to accept the things I
cannot change,
Courage to change the things I
can, and
the wisdom to know the difference.
Living one day at a time;
Enjoying one moment at a time;
Accepting hardship as the pathway
to peace.
Taking, as He did, this world as
it is, not as I would have it;
Trusting that He will make all things
right if I surrender to His will;
That I may be reasonably happy in
this life,
And supremely happy with Him
forever in the next.

—Reinhold Niebuhr

We that had loved him so, followed him, honored him,
Lived in his mild and magnificent eye,
Learned his great language, caught his clear accents,
Made him our pattern to live and to die!

—Robert Browning, The Lost Leader

Perhaps one of his beautiful children
spoke most simply and eloquently for us all.
Learning of his father's death, he said in a tone
of measureless loss, "He was so nice."
So he was. So he truly was.

—Fr. Joseph Gallagher,
for his brother, Francis Xavier Gallagher

*M*y tears flow as I write this. But even in death, Dad still teaches me. He has left me a legacy of honesty, family, love and honor. He encourages me to guide my life with grace and dignity. He leads me with the memories of his humor, kindness and courage. Thank you, Dad. Thank you for all you gave me here on earth and for all you continue to give me from your place on high. I miss you so much.... I still listen for that sweet sound of your whistle coming to my door. I will carry on, Dad. I will make you proud. I will raise your grandchildren to be as you are. A man to remember, a man to honor in death as in life. Be listening for me, Dad. I will be listening for you.

—Tami Richard, for her father, Carlos Bruce Miller

You remain my father,
philosopher, counselor
and friend.

—A Son's Prayer

🍂

He taught me to run high on my toes.
I will always remember his words:
"Run proud and remember you are alive."

—Brian Andreas, "Still Mostly True"

🍂

All these years later,
I still hear your gentle laughter,
still feel your love, still see your light.

—Helen Marm, "In Touch With Dad"

When I was with my father,
when I was just a child,
the world was filled with wonder
and every place was wild.
And every day was magic,
and Santa Claus was true,
and all the things that mattered
were things my father knew.
We often went exploring...
and I learned to love the land,
but the greatest thing I ever learned
was how to understand—
That the finest gifts are often
things we may not always see;
when I wasn't with my father,
my father was with me.

— Marsha Jeffrey Hendrickson, Thanatos Magazine

$\mathcal{M}$y bags are packed and I am ready to go.

— Pope John XXIII

🍂

$\mathcal{D}$eath is not a journeying into
an unknown land; it is a voyage home.
We are not going to a strange country,
but to our Father's house, and among
our kith and kin.

— John Ruskin

🍂

$\mathcal{W}$hen Christ ascended
Triumphantly,
from star to star,
He left the gates of heaven ajar.

— Henry Wadsworth Longfellow

The church is full. Many faces are unknown to me; others are mileposts of my years. I take a deep breath and pray, one last time for strength and composure, and deliver his eulogy. At the end, I borrowed the words of a friend who'd walked this path before: "Daddy," she wrote, "just follow the heading Peter Pan gave to Wendy Darling. As they surveyed the stars spread across the night sky, he showed her the way like you have shown me: 'Second star to the right, then straight on 'til morning.' Have a wonderful flight. We'll all meet you there."

—Tad Bartimus, for her father, James L. Bartimus

I cannot forget my mother.
Though not as sturdy as others, she was my bridge.
When I needed to get across, she steadied herself
long enough for me to run across safely.

—Renita Weems

The presence of her absence
is everywhere.

—Edna St. Vincent Millay,
from a letter she wrote after her mother's death

My mother is gone, but her legacy
lives on in the person that I am and what I can be.
Love doesn't die when a loved one passes—
it is always held in your heart, a precious gift.

—Jennifer Gray, Thanatos Magazine

Adjusting to losing her, there is another, unexpected process under way as well. Where once I would not have stopped to notice, now when I look in the mirror, I see my mother's face in mine. I hear the soft, distinctive pace of her footsteps as I climb the stairs, feel the rhythm of her hands as I pick up my knitting at the end of the day. The unmistakable pitch and tone of her laughter rings out and surprises me when my children and I play happily together. Some of her returns, slowly but surely reclaiming a place in our lives.

—Julie Huston,
on her mother, Rutheda Hunt D'Alton

My candle burns at both ends;
It will not last the night;
But, ah, my foes, and, oh, my friends—
It gives a lovely light.

—Edna St. Vincent Millay

Thank you for all the love you gave me.
There could be no one stronger.
Thank you for the many beautiful songs.
They will live long and longer.

—Epitaph for Hank Williams

Forever
Remember

74

wish you would mention the joy she had for life. That's what she gave me. If she was the tragic figure they say she was, I would be a wreck, wouldn't I? It was her love that carried her through everything. The middle of the road was never for her. It bored her. She wanted the pinnacle of excitement. If she was happy, she wasn't just happy. She was ecstatic. And, when she was sad, she was sadder than anyone. She lived eighty lives in one. And yet, I thought she would outlive us all. She was a great talent and for the rest of my life, I will be proud to be her daughter.

— Liza's farewell at Judy Garland's memorial service,
  Under the Rainbow: The Real Liza Minnelli

$\mathcal{I}$ see skies of blue, and clouds of white
Bright blessed days, and dark sacred nights
And I think to myself, 'What a wonderful world.'

I see friends shaking hands—'How do you do?'
They're really saying, 'I love you.'
And I think to myself, 'What a wonderful world.'

I hear babies cry, and I watch them grow
They'll learn much more than I'll ever know.
And I think to myself, 'What a wonderful world.'

I see trees of green, red roses too
I see them bloom, for me and for you.
And I think to myself, 'What a wonderful world.'

— Weiss & Theile,
"What A Wonderful World"

Forever Remembered

76

"What a Wonderful World," sung by Louis Armstrong, was always a favorite song of my mother's. So when she died seven years ago, we chose to have the song played at her funeral. It was somewhat of a departure from the usual hymn or ballad, but the impact it had on all who attended was unforgettable. Everyone felt touched and comforted. We had all wanted my mother's funeral to be not only a time to say good-bye, but a time to celebrate her life and the wonderful spirit she possessed. I don't know of a song that could have conveyed these messages more beautifully or clearly.

— Beth Bingham

As long as I can
I will look at this world
for both of us.
As long as I can
I will laugh with the birds,
I will sing with the flowers,
I will pray to the stars,
for both of us.
As long as I can
I will remember
how many things
on this earth

were your joy.
And I will live
as well as you
would want me to live
As long as I can.

—Sascha,
"For Both of Us," Wintersun

A letter to my twin:

I promise, Marlene, to try my best to live life to its fullest—after all, I feel that I now must laugh, play, talk, and enjoy for both of us. I'll carry a part of you, my twin, with me every moment and every hour of my life.... I'll cherish those times we jointly created, so you will never be more than just a wonderful memory away from my heart. And most importantly, my beloved twin, I'll never stop loving you. I'll thank God every single day for having blessed me with your presence in my life. Until we meet again and laugh and smile once more, know that I shall love you always!

—Arlene Carrol Matthews, twin of Marlene Carrol, Twinless Twins Support Group Newsletter

My big brother was so good to me.
When we were kids, he always let me go first.
The night he died, he looked up at me,
smiled his little crooked smile, and said,
"Sis, this time let me go first."

—Connie Danson,
eulogy for her brother, Frank Darnell

In one of the stars, I shall be living,
In one of them, I shall be laughing,
and so it will be as if all the stars
were laughing when you look
at the sky at night.

—The Little Prince,
Antoine de Saint-Exupery

I'm loving you, I know you're there
Yet I'm not sure where you are.
Are you sitting here beside me,
or were you the bird that flew?
I feel the wind blow in my ears,
and I'm wondering if it's you.
Are you reading over my shoulder?
Are you holding my hand right now?
I want to tell you I love you,
I'm not sure if I know just how.
I can feel you wiping my teardrops,
and asking me, please, not to cry.
But I'm missing you, loving
you so much. And I'm wondering why
you had to die.

— Brandy Sively Portera, for her brother Brent,
Thanatos Magazine

I shall hear in Heaven.

—Ludwig van Beethoven

E arth has no sorrow
that Heaven cannot heal.

—Sir Thomas Moore

D eath is no more than
passing from one room into another.
But there's a difference for me, you know.
Because in that other room
I shall be able to see.

—Helen Keller,
from Pat Wicks, Hospice

God saw you were getting tired
    And a cure was not to be,
    So he put His arms around you
    And whispered, "Come with me."

    With tearful eyes we watched you suffer
    And saw you fade away.
    Although we loved you dearly
    We could not make you stay.

    A 'golden heart' stopped beating,
    Working hands put to rest;
    God broke our hearts to prove to us,
    He only takes the Best.

    — Unknown

$\mathcal{D}$o you suppose
that when grandma dies
more of her stays than goes?

—Paula Gunn Allen,
"Grandma's Dying Poem"

$\mathcal{T}$hose who love deeply
never grow old; they may die of old age,
but they die young.

—Arthur Wing Pinero

$\mathcal{Y}$ou never thought of her as being old.
She had a girlish sparkle right till
the end of her life.

—Bruce Beresford,
remembering actress Jessica Tandy

It was a few months after my grandmother's death that I was taking a course in creative writing. My teacher suggested that I record some of my thoughts to help me work through my sadness. This diary became my memorial to her. Even now I read aloud the pages. I still laugh and cry about times we shared together.

—Earl A. Grollman,
Time Remembered

That best portion of a good man's life,
His little, nameless, unremembered acts
of kindness and of love.
— *William Wordsworth*

Because he lived,
there is more love in the world than
there would have been without him.
And for him, that was the reason above
all others for the gift of life.
— *New York Times, a tribute to Martin Buber*

There is a land of the living and
a land of the dead and the bridge is love,
the only survival, the only meaning.
— *Thornton Wilder,*
The Bridge of San Luis Rey

An old man going a lone highway
Came at the evening, cold and gray,
To a chasm vast and wide and steep,
With waters rolling cold and deep.
But he turned when safe on the other side,
And built a bridge to span the tide.
"Old Man," said a fellow pilgrim near,
"You waste your strength with building here.
Your journey will end with the ending day,
You never again will pass this way."
The builder lifted his old gray head,
"Good friend, in the path I have come,"
He said, "there followeth after me today
A youth whose feet must pass this way.
He, too, must cross in the twilight dim;
Good friend, I am building this bridge for him."

— Will Allen Dromgoole, "The Bridge Builder"

$\mathcal{S}$ome win eternal life only after
many years, others, a single hour.

—Talmud

$\mathcal{I}$ knew you for a moment,
A blest and hopeful while.
Now off you go,
And yet you'll stay forever,
My innocent child.
Hush-a-by, Hush-a-by...Bye.

—Charlene Nelson, in memory of Patrick Lee,
Share Pregnancy and Infant Loss Newsletter

*Forever
Remembered*

88

I can't say when the turning point came, but I think it must come for each of us if we let it. Every child who touches our lives, whether for a moment or for decades, has significance. We may have to search deeply for them, but the essential blessings are there—these treasures and gifts from our children. A part of them lives on when we dare to let ourselves remember, because however brief their journey through this world, our memories are proof of their existence!

—Dana Gensler, A Memory of Significance,
LARGO Newsletter

The gates of heaven are so
easily found when we are little,
and they are always standing open
to let the children wander in.
—Sir James Matthew Barrie

Never place a period
where God has placed a comma.
—Gracie Allen

I am the Resurrection.
If anyone believes in Me,
even though he dies he will live,
and whoever lives and believes
in Me will never die.
—John 11:20

Forever
Remembere

90

*M*ay I now say a word to you, the members of the bereaved families. It is almost impossible to say anything that can console you at this difficult hour and remove the deep clouds of disappointment....[But] I hope you can find some consolation from Christianity's affirmation that death is not the end. Death is not a period that ends the great sentence of life, but a comma that punctuates it to more lofty significance. Death is not a blind alley that leads the human race into a state of nothingness, but an open door which leads man into life eternal. Let this daring faith, this great invincible surmise, be your sustaining power during these trying days.

— *Martin Luther King,*
for the martyred children of Birmingham

In the deserts of the heart,
Let the healing Fountain start.

—W. H. Auden

Come together, now, it helps to sing.

—Singer Judy Collins,
to the friends and relatives of the 230 loved ones
who went down in TWA Flight 800

"Amazing grace, how sweet the sound
that saved a wretch like me
I once was lost, but now am found
Was blind, but now I see."

—John Newton, Amazing Grace

Forever
Remembere

92

It has been said that there are several ways to mourn. One is to weep; and we have done our share of weeping. Another way to mourn is to sing: to sing a hymn to life, a life that still abounds in sights and sounds and vivid colors; to sing the song our beloved no longer has the chance to sing. We sing the songs of our beloved; we aspire to their qualities of spirit; we take up their tasks as they would have shouldered them.

—Rabbi Jack Stern Jr.

My son was dead, and is alive again;
he was lost and now is found.

—*Luke* 15:24

On the heavens
in shining stars,
On the earth
in tender flowers,
The one you love
will live forever.

—*Jean Paul Richter*

For is it not as if
the rose that climbed
My garden wall had bloomed
the other side?

—*Alice Cary*

Danny, our only child, passed away at the age of twelve. His death was unexpected, and the pain almost unbearable. Our pastor told us that yellow is the color of life. What then could be more fitting than yellow roses? To ensure these symbols of life for years to come, I bought a rose bush for my wife. After all, she was still Danny's mom and needed more than ever to be reminded of that. I planted the bush on Mother's Day. On the day before Father's Day, the roses bloomed—three of them, to be exact. They were arranged in size order, just as our family had been in life. When I bought the bush, there was no way to know that there were to be only three roses. I have no doubt this was a sign from Danny. He wanted us to know that he still lives, and that there are still three roses.

—John W. Carlsen, Bereavement Magazine

We believe that lives are
measured in memories, not years.

— Make-A-Wish Foundation

The spirit is a wonderful thing.
I had my son in my life for 14 years.
That's a blessing: that I had the chance to hold
him, help him grow and see him smile.

— Mary Wilson, one of the original Supremes,
recalling the death of her son, Rafael

On the seashore of endless worlds
the children meet with shouts and dances.

—Rabindranath Tagore

Love shared with our cherished, only child, Lisa Marie Champlin, endures. We whisper "Lisa"—she appears in a butterfly's dance, the kiss of a gentle breeze or soft Spring rain. Her love surrounds and inspires us. She maintained her grace, dignity, and wacky sense of humor through years of living with brain cancer. We envision her free from all encumbrances—running like the horses she loved, sight restored, hair flying. Lisa, what a gift that you are our daughter!

—Linda Nielsen, Founder of In Loving Memory, and Lisa's Mom

E ver been the best of friends!
—*Charles Dickens*

🍃

I remember you lying on the bed
reading and eating green apples
the kind that crunch with each munch
Spartan...MacIntosh...Granny Smith

for years I couldn't start a book
without going through the same ritual

when I visited the cemetery
others had put pebbles on the gravestones
to mark they had been there
I left you a hard green apple
—*Renee Rodin, Bread and Salt*

Did I love you? Surely yes.

Did you know? Absolutely.

Was it enough? Never.

Is it over? Yes, forever.

Will it end? Not ever.

I bid you good-bye and love you still,

Dancing in the joy of what we had.

Crying in its loss, praying for your soul.

Not knowing if you need it.

But believing it is a link.

—Clarice Hausch, Bereavement Magazine

It is a great thing to know that when the eternal doors swing wide open the other way for you, you have a friend on the other side waiting to receive you.

—Howard Kelly

Life! We've been long together
Through pleasant and
through cloudy weather;
'Tis hard to part when friends are dear—
perhaps 'twill cost a sigh, a tear;
Then steal away, give little warning,
Choose thine own time;
Say not good-night,
but in some brighter clime
Bid me good-morning.

—Anna Letitia Barbauld

*G*ood-bye to you, my trusted friend;
  we've known each other since
  we were nine or ten.
Together we climbed hills and trees,
learned of love and ABC's,
skinned our hearts and skinned our knees.

Good-bye my friend, it's hard to die
when all the birds are singing in the sky.
Now that spring is in the air,
pretty flowers everywhere,
think of me and I'll be there.

— McKuen & Brel,
  "Seasons in the Sun"

And the song,
from beginning to end,
I found again
in the heart of a friend.

—Henry Wadsworth Longfellow

I loved my friend
He went away from me
There's nothing more to say
The poem ends soft as it began—
I loved my friend.

—Langston Hughes

One came and told me suddenly,
   "Your friend is Dead! last year she went,"
But many years my friend had spent
In life's wide wastes, apart from me.
And lately I had felt her near,
   And walked as if by soft winds fanned,
Had felt the touching of her hand,
Had known she held me close and dear.
And swift I learned that being dead
Meant rather being free to live,
And free to seek me, free to give,
And so, my heart was comforted.

— Margaret Sangster,
   "My Heart Was Comforted"

$\mathcal{W}$hen you grow old or ill,
the most important things to you will be
who and what you've loved.

—June Martin

$\mathcal{T}$he illness caused all the greatness in her
to rise to the surface. What I loved about her is
that when somebody is so much on the edge of life,
you only say the truth to them, and they only say
the truth to you. I'd like to live as she did—
diving at every day and grabbing joy
wherever you can.

—Actress Mary Steenburgen,
remembering AIDS activist, Elizabeth Glaser

Forever
Remembere

104

It has been said that my life has treated me harshly; and sometimes I have complained in my heart because so many pleasures of human experience have been withheld from me. But when I recollect the treasure of friendship that has been bestowed upon me, I withdraw all charges against life. If much has been denied me, much, very much has been given me. So long as the memory of certain beloved friends lives in my heart, I shall say that life is good.

—Hellen Keller,
   on the death of her friend, Mark Twain

$\mathscr{I}$ count myself in nothing else so happy
As in a soul remembering my good friends.

— *William Shakespeare*

$\mathscr{A}$ true friend is the
gift of God, and He who made
those hearts can unite them.

—*Robert Smith*

$\mathscr{F}$rom the first time I met the little girl
until her death recently,
a period of a little over seventy years,
we were friends.

— *Mrs. Mary E. Ackley*

Forever
Remembered

To this day, I still don't feel that she's gone.
She has real sticking power with me...
there's something about Colleen's
presence that always makes me feel
like I just saw her not too long ago.
Colleen's still very much a part of me.
There is a way you love some people
that is much stronger than having to
have them present. They become part
of your family, family in the largest,
yet most intimate, sense.

—Jason Robards,
Colleen Dewhurst: Her Autobiography

I have been trying to make
the best of grief and am just beginning to learn
to allow it to make the best of me.

—*Barbara Lazear Ascher*

I talked with mothers who had lost a child to
cancer. Every single one said death gave their
lives new meaning and purpose. And who do
you think prepared them for the rough, lonely
road they had to travel? Their dying child.
They pointed their mothers toward the future
and told them to keep going.
The children had already accepted what their
mothers were fighting to reject.

—*Erma Bombeck*

Because of you, I love a little more.
Because of you, I take time
to give an extra kiss good-bye.
Because of you, I have a new favorite song.
Because of you, there may be dust
on the window sill,
and I don't care.

Because of you, I live today,
before I worry about tomorrow.
Because of you, I don't give up quite as fast.
Because of you, I still believe in rainbows.
Because of you, now I can help or listen more.
Because of you, today, I am me.

—Eileen Wernsman,
Loving Arms Newsletter

We talk about Heaven being so far away.
It is within speaking distance.

—*Dwight L. Moody*

Think of stepping on shore, and finding it
Heaven!
Of taking hold of a hand, and finding it
God's hand,
Of breathing new air, and finding it
celestial air,
Of feeling invigorated, and finding it
immortality,
Of passing from storm and tempest to an
unbroken calm,
Of waking up, and finding it
Home!

—*Unknown*

As a boy I thought of Heaven as a glorious golden city, with nobody in it but angels, and they were all strangers to me. When my little brother died, then I thought of Heaven as that great city, full of angels, with just one little fellow in it. Then my acquaintances began to die, and the number of my friends in Heaven grew larger. But, it was not until one of my own little ones was taken that I began to feel a personal interest in Heaven. Now so many of my friends and loved ones have gone there, that it seems I know more in Heaven than on earth. Now, when my thoughts turn to Heaven, it is not the gold walls I think of—but the loved ones there. It is not the place so much as the company that makes Heaven seem beautiful.

— Unknown

$\mathcal{E}$arth is crammed with Heaven.

—Elizabeth Barrett Browning

$\mathcal{G}$od has made of death
a narrow, starlit strip between the
companionships of yesterday and
the reunions of tomorrow.

— William Jennings Bryan

$\mathcal{T}$here is no end.
There is no beginning. There is only
the infinite passion of life.

—Federico Fellini

If I should ever leave you whom I love
To go along the Silent Way, grieve not,
Nor speak of me with tears, but laugh and talk
Of me as if I were beside you there.
And when you hear a song or see a bird
I loved, please do not let the thought of me
Be sad...For I am loving you just as
I always have...You were so good to me!
There are so many things I wanted still
To do—so many things to say to you...
Remember that I did not fear...It was
Just leaving you that was so hard to face...
We cannot see beyond, but this I know.
I loved you so— 'twas heaven here with you!

—Isla Paschal Richardson, "To Those I Love"

There is no place love is not.

Hugh Prather,
In God's Care

In a dream I walked with God
through the wondrous expanse of creation,
past every sweet stirring of life and
into an infinity that breathed as
I breathe, that set the tiny
alongside the magnificent,
sparkling and shimmering in delight
of its own oneness. And there,
snug between the splendid spirits
of every earthly love, was you.

— Molly Fumia, Safe Passage

Do not stand at my grave and weep,
I am not there, I do not sleep.

I am a thousand winds that blow,
I am the softly falling snow.
I am the gentle showers of rain,
I am the fields of ripening grain.

I am in the morning hush,
I am in the graceful rush
Of beautiful birds in circling flight.
I am the starshine of the night.

I am in the flowers that bloom,
I am in a quiet room.
I am in the birds that sing,
I am in each lovely thing.

Do not stand at my grave and cry,
I am not there—I did not die.

— Unknown

The dead don't die.
They look on and help.

—D.H. Lawrence

In dreams he comes to me.
"I am well, if you need me,
I am here."
I wake feeling loved,
more whole than before....
My father returns from death,
bearing gifts
life denied both of us.

— Mitzi Chandler,
It's Never Too Late

I am standing upon the seashore. A ship at my side spreads her white sails to the morning breeze and starts for the blue ocean. She is an object of beauty and stregnth, and I stand and watch until at last she hangs like a speck of white cloud just where the sea and sky come down to mingle with each other. Gone where? Gone from my sight is all. She is just as large and beautiful as when she left my side. Her diminished size is in me, not in her. And just at the moment when someone at my side says, "There she goes!" there are other eyes watching her coming and other voices ready to take up the glad shout, "Here she comes!"

— Henry Van Dyke

In the night of death, hope sees a star and listening love can hear the rustle of a wing.

—Robert Ingersoll

I'll keep finding things
that are important,
and I'll know you put them there.
In life, you made my life complete;
in death, you've left me life's intent.
Your love was wondrously given...
not to be saved, but spent.

—Janet Vaughan, for Denice,
Bereavement Magazine

To the living I am gone,
To the sorrowful, I will never return,
To the angry I was cheated.
But to the happy, I am at peace.
And to the faithful, I have never left.
I cannot speak, but I can listen.
I cannot be seen, but I can be heard.
So as you stand upon a shore,
gazing at a beautiful sea,
Remember Me....
Remember Me in your heart, in your thoughts,
and the memories of the times we loved,
the memories of the time we shared.
For if you always think of Me,
I will have never gone.

— Unknown

Your loved one may be gone,
but the relationship lives on.

—Kelly Ann Rothaus

Yet love will dream, and Faith will trust
That somehow, somewhere, meet we must.
Life is ever lord of Death
And Love can never lose its own.

—John Greenleaf Whittier

What we call the end is also a beginning.
The end is where we start from.

—T.S. Eliot

Finally one night it happened. We came together once more in a dream to say good-bye. It was something that had been left out, and for a long time I had searched for a better ending. It was so much more than a good-bye. It was many things at once, memories and stories and celebration. And when it was time to part, it was hardly an ending, but a blessing, really, of everything we continue to be to each other. Perhaps there will be another dream someday. And our conversation will continue, without a beginning or an end, as it is with love.

— Molly Fumia, Safe Passage

$\mathcal{R}$ecall as often as you wish;
a happy memory never wears out.

— *Libbie Fudim*

$\mathcal{W}$here there is pain,
let there be softening.
Where there is bitterness,
let there be acceptance.
Where there is silence,
let there be communication.
Where there is loneliness,
let there be friendships.
Where there is despair,
let there be hope....

— *Ruth Eiseman,*
Loving Arms Newsletter

Forever
Remembered

I wish I could tell everyone who has lost a loved one how important it is to let themselves, and their family, remember. Forget, if you can, the sickness, or tragedy that took them, but give them a place in your life. My family speaks very naturally of their father and their sister. We remember the fun, the love, and the closeness.... We have memories to cherish, and we shouldn't cheat ourselves by not doing that. I don't mean that we should constantly talk about them, but when something we're doing reminds us of something good that happened when we were still a whole family, we don't hesitate to say so.

— Lettie Petrie, Bereavement Magazine

At the rising of the sun and its going down,
We remember them.
At the blowing of the wind and in the chill of winter,
We remember them.
At the opening of the buds and in the rebirth of spring,
We remember them.
At the rustling of the leaves and in the beauty of autumn,
We remember them.
At the beginning of the year and when it ends,
We remember them.
As long as we live, they too will live.
They are part of us,
We remember them.

—Gates of Prayer

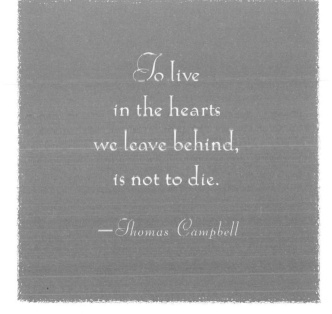

To live
in the hearts
we leave behind,
is not to die.

—Thomas Campbell

With Sincere Appreciation

The editors would like to express our appreciation and admiration to the following bereavement support groups and resources for their inspiration, contributions, or assistance.

The National Directory of Bereavement Support Groups and Services. Mary M. Wong, Editor. ADM Publishing, (718) 657-1277.

Bereavement Magazine, 8133 Telegraph Drive, Colorado Springs, CO 80920. (719) 282-1948. A magazine of hope and healing.

Concerns of Police Survivors (COPS), P.O. Box 3199, Camdenton, MO. 65020. (314) 346-4911. Reaching out to help America's police survivors.

Friends for Survival, Inc., P.O. Box 214463, Sacramento, CA. 95821. (916) 392-0664. An outreach program for survivors of suicide loss.

Hospice of Kitsap County, P.O. Box 3416, Silverdale, WA. 98383. Provides quality physical, emotional, and spiritual care for the terminally ill.

In Loving Memory, 1416 Green Run Lane, Reston, VA. 22090. (703) 435-0608. A support group for parents with no surviving children.

LARGO, Life After Repeated Grief Options, 1192 South Uvalda Street, Aurora, CO. 80013. (303) 745-1799. For parents who have had more than one child die.

Our House: A Bereavement Center, 1554 S. Sepulveda, Suite #107, Los Angeles, CA. 90025. (310) 444-0440.

Parents of Murdered Children, Inc., 100 East Eighth Street, #B-41, Cincinnati, OH. 45202. (513) 721-5683. For the families and friends of those who have died by violence.

Pregnancy and Infant Loss Center, 1421 E. Wayzata Blvd. #30, Wayzata, MN. 55391. (612) 473-9372. Support, resources, and education on miscarriage, stillbirth, and infant death. Publishes Loving Arms Newsletter.

Ray of Hope, Inc., P. O. Box 2323, Iowa City, IA. 52244. (319) 337-9890.
Concerned with survivors of suicide and their grief process.

Safe Passage: Words to Help the Grieving Hold Fast and Let Go.
Molly Fumia, author. Berkeley: Conari Press, 1992.

San Diego Hospice, 4311 Third Avenue, San Diego, CA. 92103.
(619) 688-1500. Provides quality physical, emotional, and spiritual care
for the terminally ill.

SCI (Service Corporation International), 1929 Allen Parkway, Houston, TX.
77019, (713) 522-5141. Provides caring funeral and cemetery services to
families in 2,000 communities worldwide.

SHARE Pregnancy and Infant Loss Support, Inc., St. Joseph Health Center,
300 First Capitol Drive, St. Charles, MO. 63301. (314) 947-6164. Support
following the death of a baby through miscarriage, ectopic pregnancy,
stillbirth or neonatal death.

Thanatos Magazine, P. O. Box 6009, Tallahassee, FL. 32314. (904) 224-1969.
A realistic journal concerning dying, death & bereavement.

THEOS Foundation, 322 Boulevard of the Allies, Suite 105, Pittsburgh, PA.
15222. (412) 471-7779. Provides support for those who are newly widowed.

Tom Golden's Crisis, Grief, & Healing web page. http://www.webhealing.com

Twinless Twins Support Group International, 11220 St. Joe Road, Fort
Wayne, IN. 46835. (210) 627-5414. Founded to support twins and all multiple
births who suffer from the loss of their twin.

UNITE, Inc., 7600 Central Avenue, Philadelphia, PA. 19111-2499.
(215) 728-3777. A support group for parents who have experienced
miscarriage, stillbirth, or infant death.

Wintersun: Thoughts of Comfort and Understanding for Healing from Grief.
Sascha, author. LARGO, Inc., 1996

Also available from Compendium Publishing are these spirited and compelling companion books of great quotations.

Be Happy.
Remember to live, love,
laugh and learn.

Because of You™
Celebrating the Difference
You Make™

Brilliance™
Uncommon Voices From
Uncommon Women™

I Believe in You™
To your heart, your dream and
the difference you make

Little Miracles™
To renew your dreams, lift your
spirits, and strengthen your resolve™

Reach for the Stars™
Give up the Good to Go
for the Great

Thank You
In appreciation of you,
and all that you do

Together We Can™
Celebrating the power of
a team and a dream™

To Your Success™
Thoughts to Give Wings to
Your Work and Your Dreams™

Whatever It Takes™
A Journey into the Heart
of Human Achievement™

You've Got a Friend™
Thoughts to Celebrate
the Joy of Friendship™

These books may be ordered directly from the publisher (800) 914-3327.
But please try your bookstore first!

www.compendiuminc.com